Copyright © 2020 by Tom Burns ©

All rights reserved. This book or any portion thereof may not be reproduced or used in any manner whatsoever without the express written consent of the publisher except for the use of brief quotations in a book review.

Printed in the United States of America

First Printing, 2020

ISBN 9798668252152

Independently Published with Kindle Direct Publishing

Book Website: CommonSense-IThink.com

BRING BACK COMMON SENSE

PLEASE

"THE LACK OF IT"

YOU EVER WONDER...
- ***Why things are not always going well for you???
- ***Why your career is not moving in the right direction???
- ***Why your job is going nowhere???
- ***Why you are having family problems (with other relationships)???
- ***And, why many, many people cannot handle the way things are going on in the world today???

MAYBE YOU ARE LACKING COMMON SENSE, OR NOT USING IT PROPERLY

YOU EVER WONDER...
- ***Why you are doing so good when others are not???
- ***Why you are being successful in your own way???
- ***Why you are respected, both in your business life as well as in your personal life???
- ***Why you are in a position to help others???
- ***And, why you are able to control things in life while the rest of the world around you is going to hell in a hand-basket???

MAYBE IT'S BECAUSE YOU ARE USING YOUR COMMON SENSE PROPERLY.

WELL, I RECKON IT'S SOMETHING TO THINK ABOUT...

Tom Burns

ONE OLD STORY:

ONE OLD STORY WITH A NEW BEGINNING

I'm going to be talking about you...perhaps.

I bet you are the type of person who, either wants to be better in life or really planning to do better in life. Well, you are not alone.

No matter what your directions are, or your plans are, in order to do a good job at your quest, you must take COMMON SENSE along with you. And that's not too hard to do. The truth of the matter is that it is very simple. The Good Lord gave us all COMMON SENSE. We all may see it in a different light. But, we still have it. It's the way we each apply it that determines the outcome.

You do realize, when using your COMMON SENSE, you can only do it in 2 ways at the same time. For example, this is what your COMMON SENSE will tell you:

- ***COMMON SENSE will tell you what's right and what's wrong.
- ***COMMON SENSE will tell you what's good or what's bad.
- ***COMMON SENSE will tell you what you should do and what you should not do.

Now, you could stay up all night trying to improve it. But, I doubt it if you can do it.

Note: Throughout this book, when using the words COMMON SENSE, I will only be using the initials CS. It's been said, when someone looks at a picture, everyone sees something different. I hope it's so.

YOU MAY NOT WANT TO READ BOOKS.

YOU MAY NOT LIKE TO READ BOOKS.

BUT...

MAYBE YOU WOULD LOOK AT PICTURES ABOUT WHAT COMMON SENSE SHOULD BE.

*** SO LOOK ***

C/S WILL ALLOW YOU TO DO THIS, IF YOU WISH...

IF YOU ARE **BENT** ON DESTROYING YOURSELF, THE WORLD WILL LET YOU DO IT.

TIP: FOR WHAT IT'S WORTH, THAT'S NOT A GOOD IDEA...

C/S KNOWS... EVERYTHING ~~WILL~~ CHANGES.

* SOME FOR THE BAD.   *SOME FOR THE GOOD.

IF YOU USE THE 80/20 RULE, YOU CAN CONTROL MOST OF IT.

SUCCESS IS ...

... ALWAYS OUT IN FRONT OF YOU.

*MOST PEOPLE ARE JUST BLIND

Mooo!
Mooo!
Mooo!
Mooo!

COUNTRY WISDOM?

THE EARLY BIRD GETS THE WORM

DON'T BE A LOSER... GET UP WITH THE ROOSTERS

GET YOUR DUCKS IN A ROW

ROAD TO SUCCESS

"Hey, over here."

Common Sense Knows Better

Looks Like a
BIG
Checkˌ
But,

It's Still

Chicken Feed

Check text:
ABC Inc.
Everywhere USA
Pay To The Order Of: You & Your Family
Very Little Amount $ No Benifits
Bank Of Nothing
For: Making Others Wealthy
Now $ Into The Future   Date
$ Minimum Wage
Employer (Smiling)   Signed

❓ Tip: Learn Self-Education

c/s will tell you...
...celdom seen

Once You Realize Life has A lot of Misteaks in it,

Then You Got it Maid! :)

Maybee???

If you learn from them

U-NEEK, RIGHT?
(IT STILL MAKES CENTS)

Even C/S knows this to be true...
ALL PEOPLE HAVE THIS PROBLEM, MEN TOO!

contractions

"I CAN'T"
"I COULDN'T"
"I WON'T"
"I DON'T"
"I MUSTN'T"
"I SHOULDN'T"

THE LAST THING WE NEED IS A LIFE WITH "NOTS" IN THEM

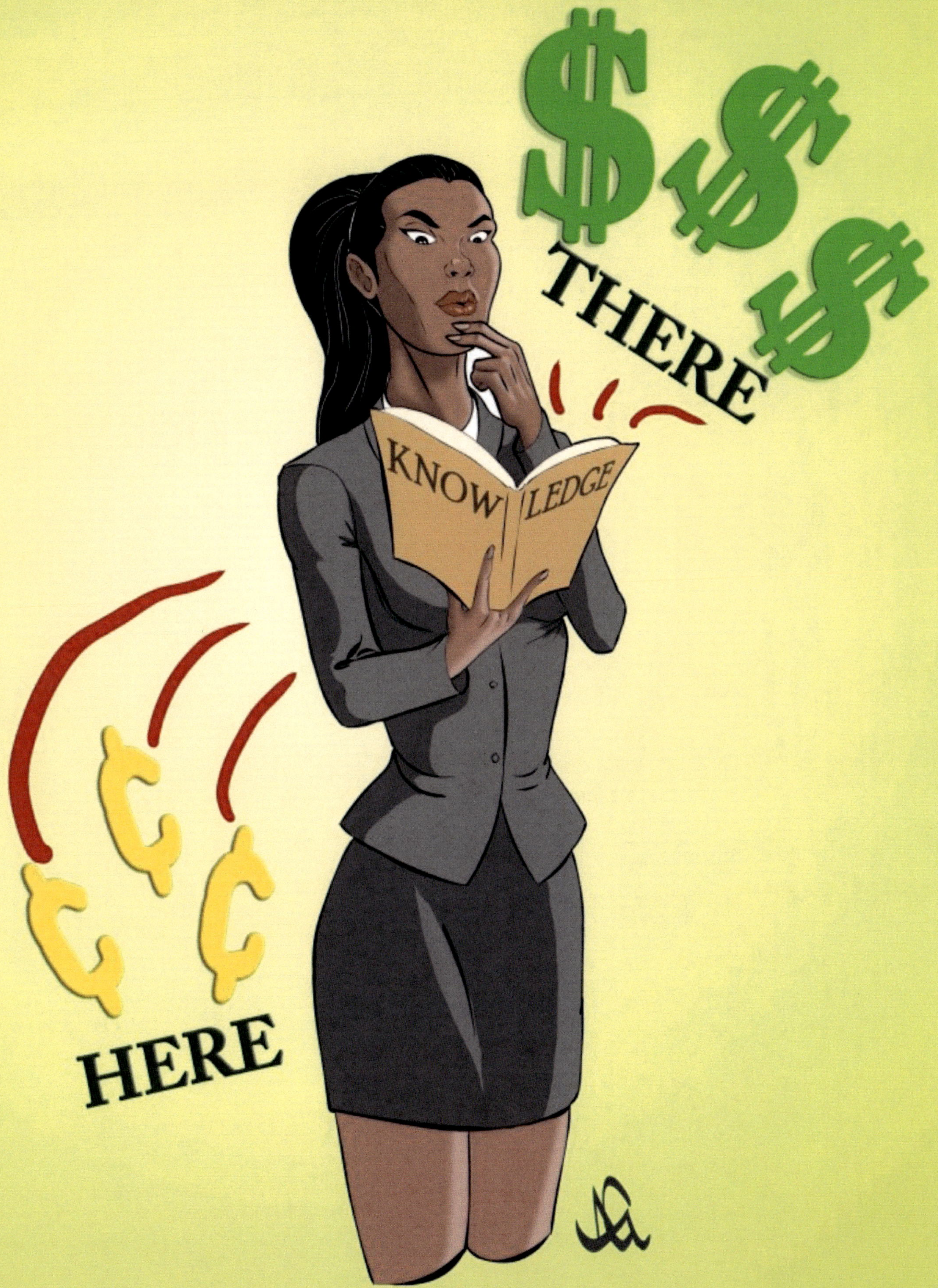
THERE
KNOW LEDGE
HERE

LOOK OUT FOR BUSINESS SHARKS

THEY ARE REAL PICKEY ON WHAT THEY EAT, THEY WILL EAT:
*YOUR DREAMS
*YOUR ATTITUDE
*YOUR HOPES
*YOUR EFFORTS

THEY WANT TO CHEW YOU UP.

IT'S HARD TO FOOL COMMON SENSE

"I WANT TO IMPROVE MYSELF"

YOU JUST MAY BE FULL OF HOT AIR

REALLY??

YOU WILL ALWAYS HAVE A SECOND CHANCE—

IT WILL BE KNOWN AS THE NEXT DAY OR TOMMOROW! SO QUIT YOUR MOANING AND GROANING AND GET WITH THE PLAN!

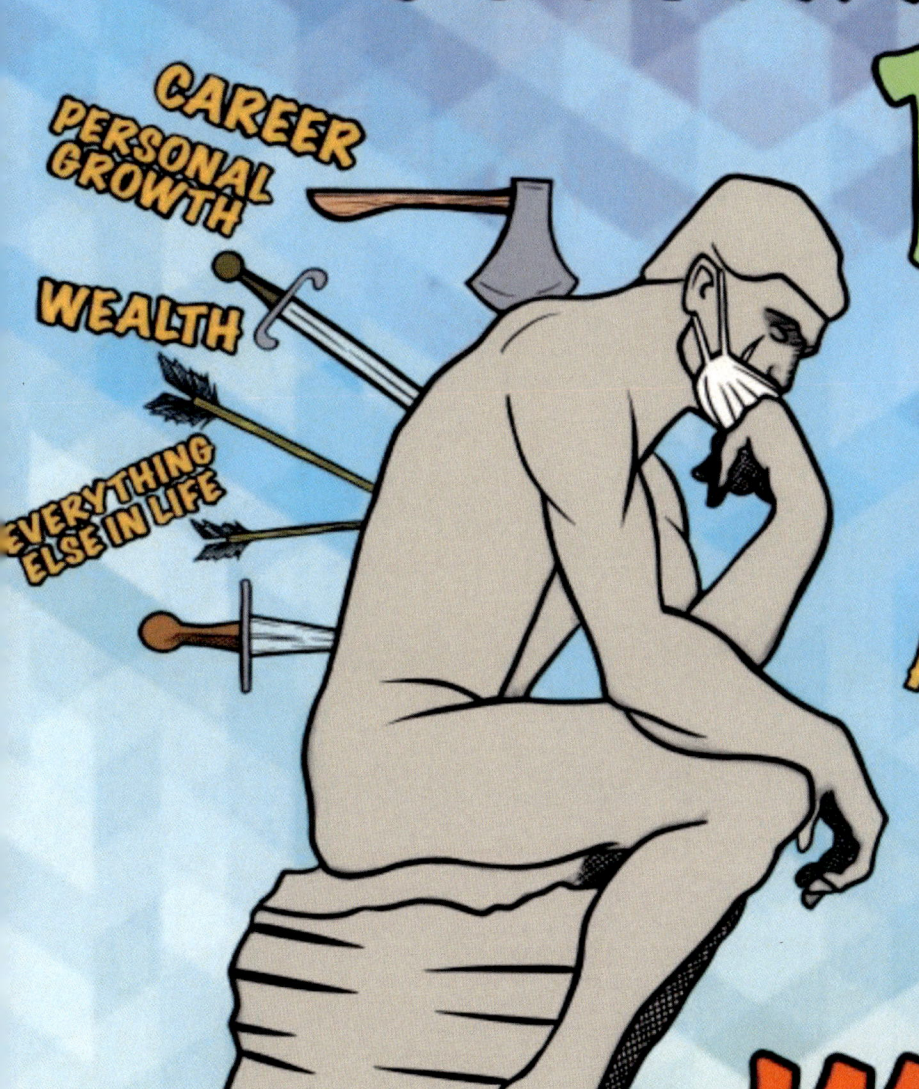

C/S WILL WARN YOU... IF ALL YOU DO IN LIFE IS THINK, AND NEVER PRODUCE ANYTHING FOR YOURSELF, WATCH OUT!!!

- CAREER
- PERSONAL GROWTH
- WEALTH
- EVERYTHING ELSE IN LIFE

C/S ALWAYS SAYS

DON'T HIDE-GO SEEK

THE GAME OF BUSINESS IS NOT A KID'S GAME

UNTIL THE MULE TRIED TO CLEAR THE FENCE... HE THOUGHT HIMSELF A ELK.

I KNOW SOME PEOPLE SEEING THEMSELVES AS ENTREPRENURS, UNTIL THEY TRY!

Sometimes You gotta....

LooKthrough

HARDSHIP

REWARDS

COMMON SENSE & MATHEMATICS
ALWAYS BE PREPARED!!!
$\nabla^2_{3D}(\chi) = A+B$
$\chi = \frac{\partial\phi}{\partial t}$
$A=-(\sigma f)\vec{V}_g\nabla(\xi_g+f)$
HIT!!!
Y+2
NOT ONLY RAIN WILL FALL ON YOU!!!

C/S
DONT SPEND TO MUCH TIME "IN THE MUD"

Sometimes People Are Like Pigs- They'll Run Their Noses Through Everything That's Negative & Fell Confortable

FEAR is just a **FEELING**

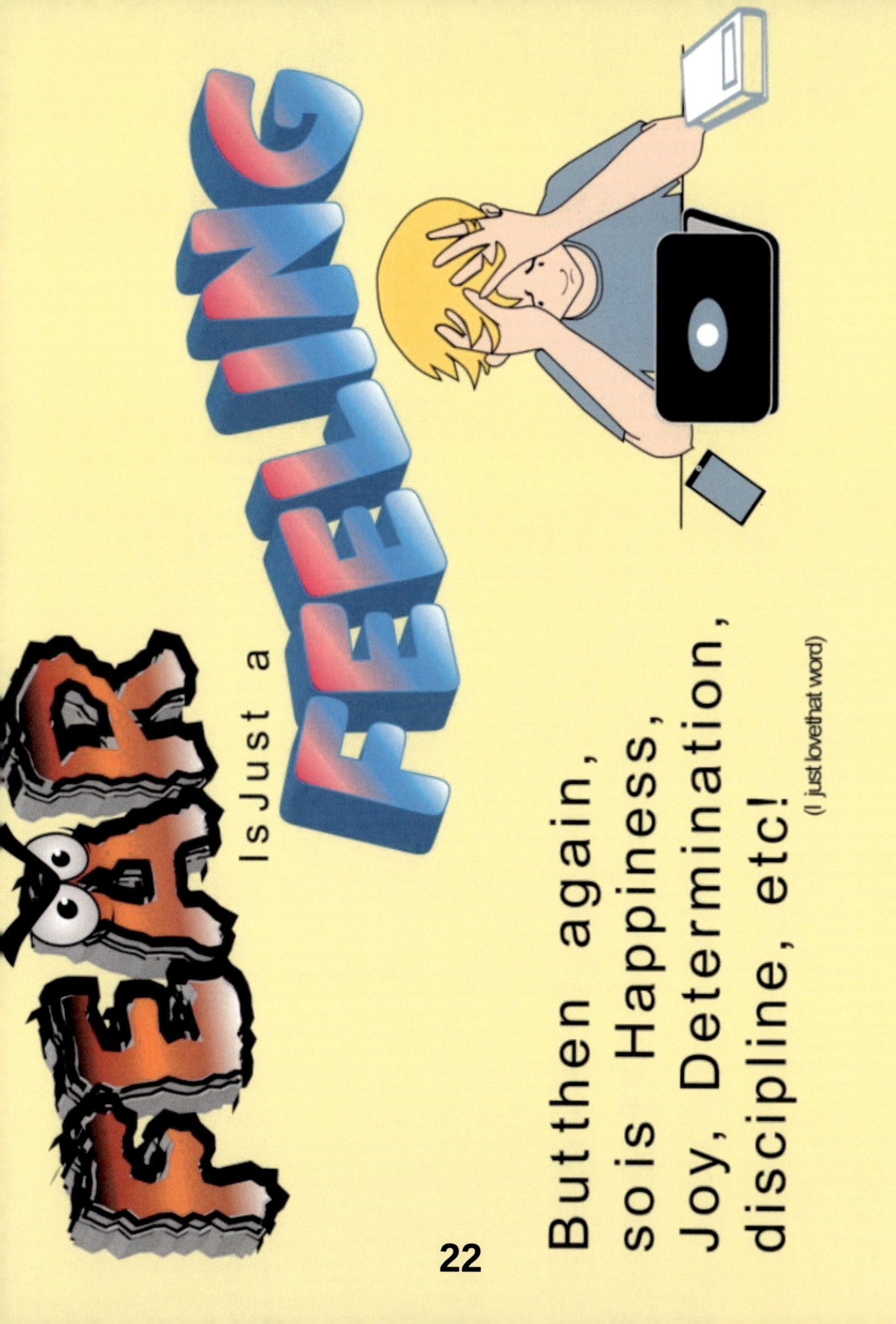

But then again, so is Happiness, Joy, Determination, discipline, etc!

(I just love that word)

C/S - KNOWS SOME PEOPLE ARE "SOME-WHAT" CONFUSED.

"I AM A ENTREPREN~~X~~ER ENTREPRE" MANURE"

THIS MAYBE WHY MANY PEOPLE ARE DOING SO POORLY!

David A.

c/s says, not everything is YOURS!

𝓚𝓵𝓮𝓹𝓽𝓸𝓶𝓪𝓷𝓲𝓪:

*The inability to resist the urge to call others ideas your own.

...Ooops

No matter how good it looks...

**If you have to be dishonest..
It's NEVER worth it**

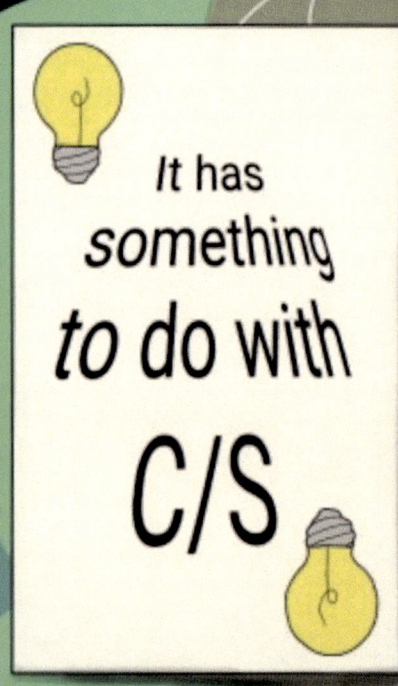

It has *something to do with* C/S

# C/S sometimes says...

Working for someone else is like trying to kick a brick through life

OUCH

Promotions

C/S wonders sometimes???

As *Shakespeare* ALMOST Put it...

"To Play To Win Or Not To Play To Win, That Is The Question"

C/S will ask,
What is "REALLY" Good Advice ???

WHEN YOU GET TO THE END OF YOUR ROPE...

TIE A KNOT & HANG ON

UNLESS YOU ARE A FEW INCHES FROM THE GROUND, THEN LET GO!

C/S IS NOT IN THIS PICTURE

DONE TRYING

NOT TODAY

SOME PEOPLE DON'T KNOW WHY THEY QUIT...

LEADERSHIP
Personal Development
FAMILY VAULES

I GIVE UP

...THAT'S WHY THEY DON'T WIN!

TB

C/S DEFINES PROCRASTINATION

OR "SOMEDAY I WILL" PHILOSOPHY

"YOU'RE NOT ALONE"

I got it figured out I'm going to start the first thing tomorrow

BEWARE!!
IF YOU CAN NOT HANDLE ME CORRECTLY
LIBERTY
1945
1¢
YOU CAN'T HANDLE MY FRIENDS CORRECTLY!!!
ME (AGAIN)
David G.

Common Sense says **There is a thing called**
Pig Wisdom

Don't have the nickname of BACON!

Be cautious of those people who are ALWAYS nice to you,,,,,
one day you're going to have to ask
WHY?

OVERTHINKING

SELF GROWTH
HEALTH
LIFE/WORK
ENTREPENEURSHIP
FAMILY
WEALTH KNOWLEDGE

C/S WILL TELL YOU 'THE ART OF CREATING PROBLEMS THAT DON'T EXIST

SOME PEOPLE WHO WANDER ARE ~~NECESSARILY~~ ABSOLUTELY LOST

C/S will ALWAYS help you put YES in SUCCESS!!

It might be misspelled...

But it's the right thing to do!!

C/S - MANY, MANY TIMES IT COMES OUT THIS WAY

YOUR BUSINESS LIFE:

IT'S NOT COMMON SENSE, IT'S NONSENSE

BEST TRY AND CHANGE

THE TRAIN TO NOWHERE

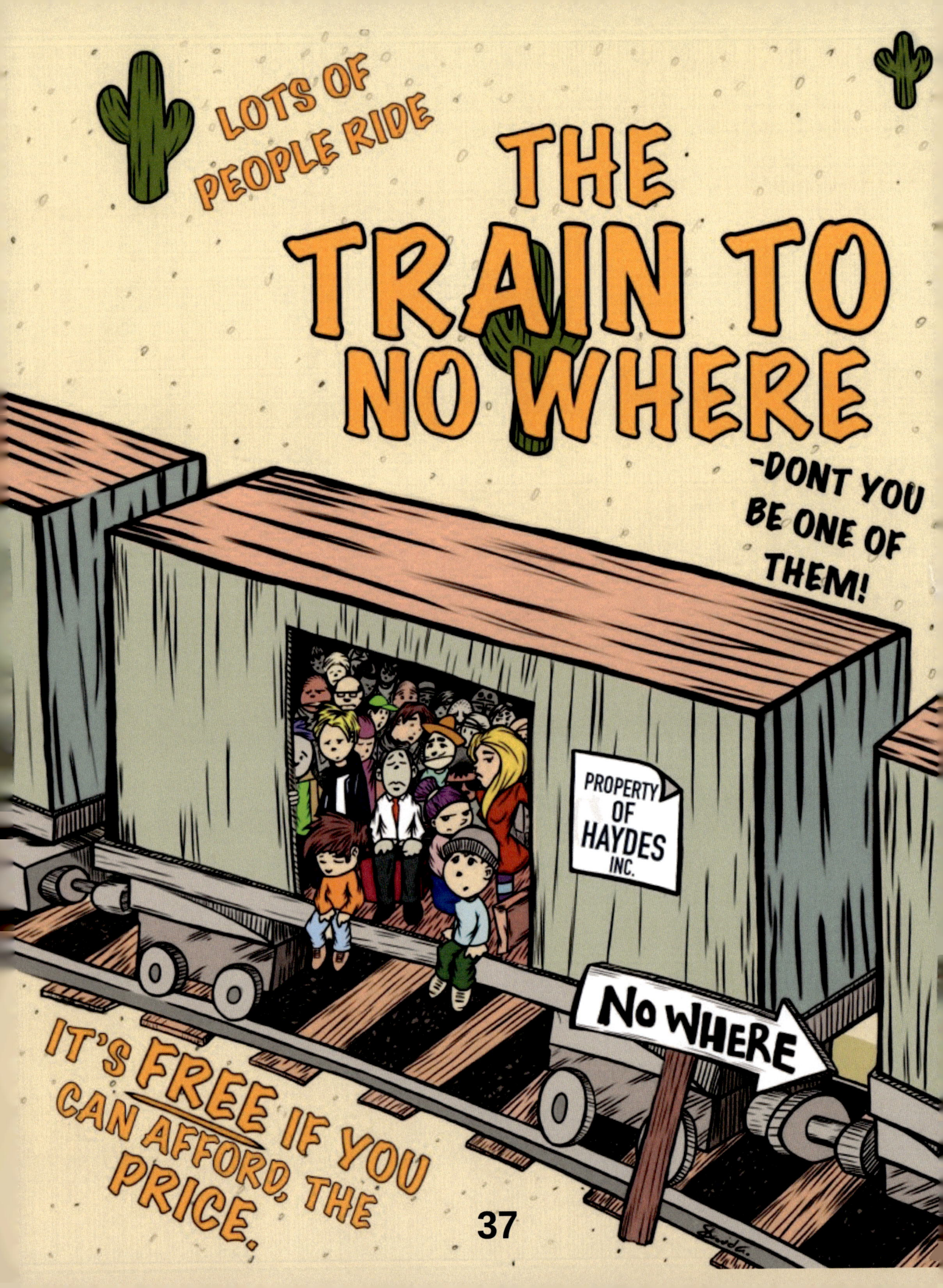

LOTS OF PEOPLE RIDE THE TRAIN TO NOWHERE

—DONT YOU BE ONE OF THEM!

PROPERTY OF HAYDES INC.

NoWHERE →

IT'S FREE IF YOU CAN AFFORD THE PRICE.

NEVER QUIT
NEVER TRYING

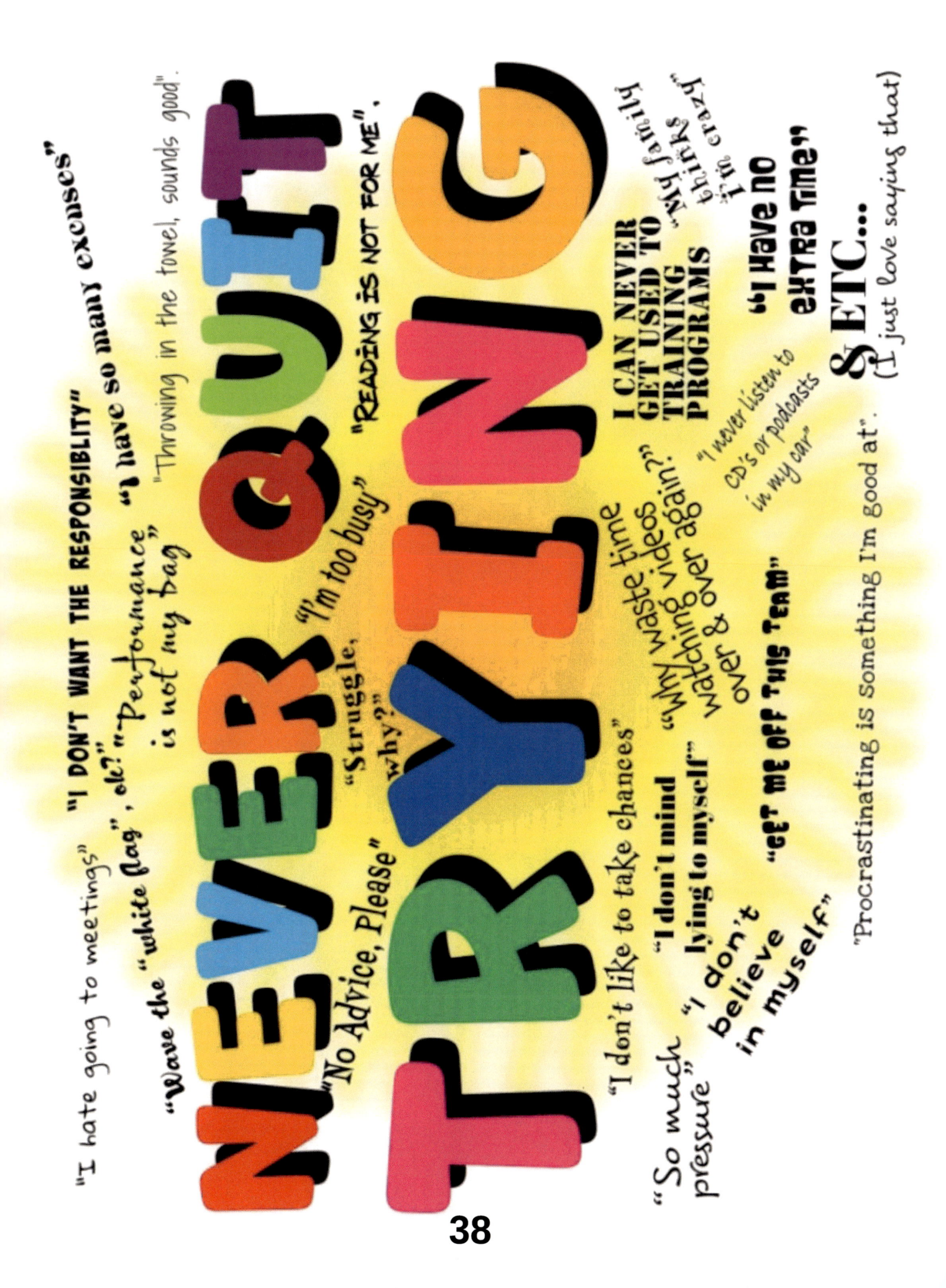

"I hate going to meetings" "I DON'T WANT THE RESPONSIBLITY" "I have so many excuses"

"Wave the "white flag", ok?" "Performance is not my bag" "Throwing in the towel, sounds good".

"No Advice, Please" "Struggle, why?" "I'm too busy" "Reading is not for me".

"So much pressure" "I don't like to take chances" "I don't mind lying to myself" "Why waste time watching videos over & over again?"

"I don't believe in myself" "GET ME OFF THIS TEAM"

"Procrastinating is something I'm good at".

I CAN NEVER GET USED TO TRAINING PROGRAMS "My family thinks I'm crazy"

"I never listen to CD's or podcasts in my car"

"I have no extra time"

& ETC... (I just love saying that)

NEVER BELIEVE !

one source of income will guarantee your future
$The Good Life

A mouse NEVER trusts its luck to one hole only!

OPPORTUNITY

I see the light

#1. You have to have the eyes to see it

It's what I want

#2. The mindset to recognize it

I CAN do it

#3. The heart to Believe it.

Now, That's using your COMMON SENSE PROPERLY!!

C/S KNOWS WHAT IT MEANS...
MISONISM

Door of OPPORTUNITY

(Now, You look up the meaning and then, You will know what it means FOREVER)

C/S says,

It only takes ONE

1000 REASONS FOR **DOING IT**

ONE REASON FOR **NOT DOING IT**

1000 REASONS FOR **NOT DOING IT**

ONE REASON FOR **DOING IT**

NOTE: YOU DO THE MATH

C/S—HERE IS WHERE PEOPLE MAKE THEIR BIGGEST **MISTAKES**

Struggle
+
Effort
+
Hardwork
=
Opportunity

"Opportunity follows struggle, it follows effort, it follows hard work, it doesn't come before." -Shelby Steale

"NAPS"

BOTH OF THEM ARE ACTUALLY NOT READING

DAY DREAMING

SOME PEOPLE, NO MATTER HOW OLD THEY GOT

THEY NEVER CHANGE.

SOME PEOPLE WILL DO EVERYTHING NECESSARY TO MAKE THEIR OWN FUTURE.

OTHERS JUST WAIT FOR SOMEONE ELSE TO MAKE THEIR FUTURE FOR THEM.

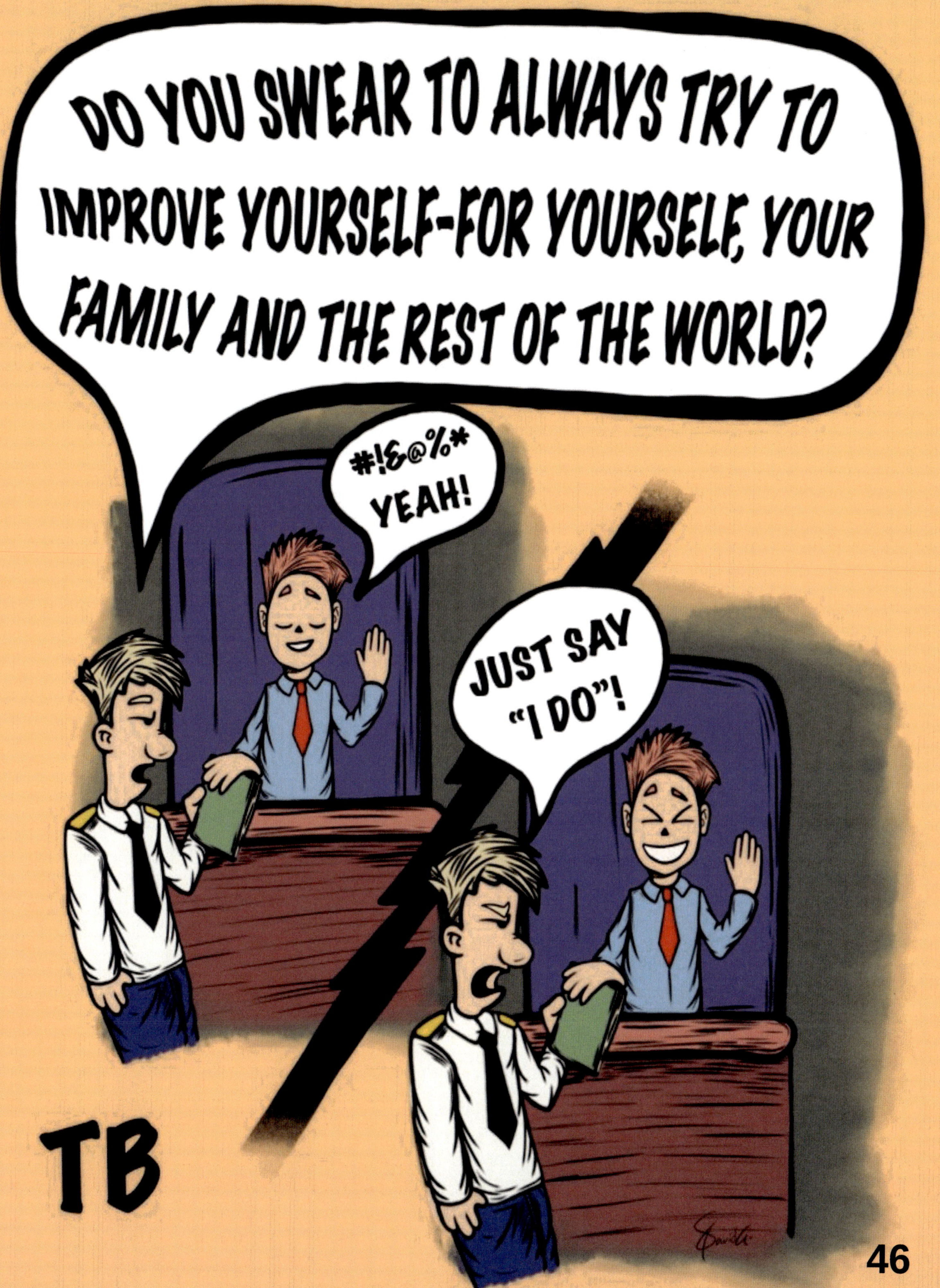

COMMON SENSE ALWAYS KNOWS:

YOU CAN ALWAYS SPOT **A LOSER** BY THE WAY THEY BEHAVE!

They seem to...

"THINK A LOT ABOUT THE PAST, AND VERY little ABOUT the Future, While in the Present"!!

What did he say?

I DONT KNOW ???

COMMON SENSE SAYS WORRY TAKES YOU DOWN A DEAD END NO OUTLET LOOK FOR OTHER AVENUES

UNAVOIDABLE
THE SUN WILL RISE AND SET

People who work hard on themselves

REWARDS COME

People who do nothing to improve themselves

NO REWARD

Note: We call this behavior a good example of COMMON SENSE!

C/S KNOWS FOR SURE-
♪ "IT'S A LONG, LONG WAY TO TIPPERARY" ♪

- Recognition
- Goals
- Ambition
- Relationships
- Accomplishments
- Self
- Money
- Possessions
- Career
- Dipolmas
- Drive
- Health
- Effort

Also, Include:
SELF-EDUCATION
HOPE-FAITH-LOVE
LEARNING / TRYING
IT'S NOT BAD TO HAVE
ENTERPRENEUR SHIP

HOORAY, YOU MADE IT- PERSONAL SUCCESS

Brother, (or Sister, too)

you can't run away

from your Self

Gospel Truth,

ain't Nobody moves

that fast

JUST AN IDEA...

...it will fit

COMMITMENT

THESE "THINGS" WILL NEVER GO TO THE PEOPLE WHO WANT THEM

THE FUTURE

"THE GOOD LIFE"
PROMOTIONS
BLESSINGS
EARNED GIFTS
RETIREMENT
BONUS
MONEY
CARRERS
REWARDS
ENTREPRENEURSHIP
MANY SUCCESESS
ACHIVEMENTS
BENEFITS

BUSINESS WORLD

THEY WILL ALWAYS GO TO THE PEOPLE WHO DESERVE THEM!!

53

DON'T FORGET THIS TYPE OF COMMON SENSE

THE HALF-TIME SCORE DOES NOT COUNT

FINISH THE GAME.

GROWTH

STEP OUTSIDE OF THE BOX FOR A GOOD REASON

COMMON SENSE BELIEVES THIS MAY BE A MAGNIFICENT LETTER IN THE BUSINESS WORLD!

SUCCESS
SERVICE • (LEARN TO BE REAL GOOD AT THIS)
SYSTEMS • (KNOW HOW IT WORKS)
STUDY • (YOU HAVE THE KNOWLEDGE, YOU ALMOST HAVE EVERYTHING)
SACRIFICE • (THE PRICE TO IMPROVE)
STAND FOR SOMETHING
SUFFER • (HARDWORK)
SATISFACTION • (KNOW YOU DID A GOOD JOB)
SELFCONFIDENCE
STUBBORN • (NEVER GIVE UP)
SELF • TAUGHT
SELF • EDUCATED
SUPERCHARGED • (FIRE IN THE BELLY)
SPIRIT
SADDNESS • (EVERY SO OFTEN THINGS GO BAD)
STUPIDITY • (SOME PEOPLE LIVE BY IT!)

C/S & GOOD ADVICE:

BE CAREFUL WITH YOUR MANNERS.

PEOPLE ARE ALWAYS WATCHING.

TB.

WIIFM?

(WHAT'S IN IT FOR ME?)
ANSWER:
"EVERYTHING"

ALL YOU GOT TO DO IS ...
STUDY

ALL YOU GOT TO HAVE IS ...
- DISCIPLINE
- INVOLVEMENT
- COMMITMENT

CLUE: MOST PEOPLE WILL NOT DO THIS.

C/S & WARNINGS...

SOME PEOPLE GET EXCITED STOMPING ON DREAMS.

(MAKE SURE THEIR ARE NOT YOURS!)

DID YOU KNOW?

NEGATIVE
- IDEAS
- BELIEFS
- THOUGHTS
- BEHAVIOR

CAN BE USED TO FILL YOUR HEAD & WASTE YOUR SPACE UNTIL YOU ARE DEAD

DON'T BUY INTO THAT STUFF!

******SUMMARY******

ILLUSTRATORS CONTRIBUTION

1). BOB ANDERSON..............................* Page 3.......The Lack of it.
    ALBUQUERQUE, NEW MEXICO   * Page 4......One Old Story.
                                                      * Page 5......You May Not Want To Read.

2). DAVID ALVARADO............................* FRONT PAGE.
    MEXICO   * Page 6........Road Runner.
                                                      * Page 7........Moo/Moo.
                                                      * Page 8........Country Wisdom.
                                                      * Page 11......Think.
                                                      * Page 13......Business Sharks.
                                                      * Page 17......Don't Hide/Go Seek.
                                                      * Page 18......Mule/Elk.
                                                      * Page 20......Hit.
                                                      * Page 21......Pig In Mud.
                                                      * Page 23......Entrepre"MANURE".
                                                      * Page 29......Give Up.
                                                      * Page 30......Procrastination.
                                                      * Page 31......Presidents.
                                                      * Page 33......Overthinking.
                                                      * Page 37......Train
                                                      * Page 44......Never Read.
                                                      * Page 46......Swear.
                                                      * Page 53......Snow Globe.
                                                      * Page 54......Finish The Game.
                                                      * Page 57......Manners.
                                                      * Page 58......WIIFM.
                                                      * Page 59......Stomp.
                                                      * Page 60......Did You Know.

3). NICOLE ANDERSON........................* Page 45......Octopus.
     ALBUQUERQUE, NEW MEXICO

4). SARAH ANDERSON...........................* Page 25......."5" Hearts (Acres).
   ALBUQUERQUE, NEW MEXICO   * Page 27......Shakespeare.
                                                    * Page 35......Yes.

5). BILL DULSKI ....* Page 14......Hot Air.
   RIO RANCHO, NEW MEXICO   * Page 47......Loser.
                                                    * Page 48......Worry.
                                                    * Page 55......Growth.
                                                    * Page 56......Letter "S".

6). DESI GARCIA....................................* Page 12........Knowledge.
   ALBUQUERQUE, NEW MEXICO

7). FELSHA LAPCHYRSKI.......................* Page 9.........Chicken Feed.
   MAKAWAO, HAWAII

8). TYLER OVERALL..............................* Page 6.........Bent.
   ALBUQUERQUE, NEW MEXICO   * Page 15......2nd Chance.
                                                    * Page 43......Struggle.

9). PETER MENICE................................* SELF-POTRAIT.
   CORRALES, NEW MEXICO

10). SUZANNE VIGIL..............................* Page 32......Pig Wisdom.
    ALBUQUERQUE, NEW MEXICO   * Page 39......Mouse.

11). WOODY WOODROME.....................* Page 10......Celdon Seen.
    ALBUQUERQUE, NEW MEXICO   * Page 24......Kleptomania.

12). MAUREEN "ROE" ROUCH...............* Page 2..........Common Sense Sign.
    RIO RANCHO, NEW MEXICO   * Page 11.......Contractions.
                                                    * Page 19........Hardship.
                                                    * Page 20........Fear.
                                                    * Page 26........Ouch.
                                                    * Page 28........Rope.
                                                    * Page 34........Wander.
                                                    * Page 36........Nonsense.
                                                    * Page 38.........Never Quit Trying.
                                                    * Page 40.........Opportunity.
                                                    * Page 41.........Misonism.
                                                    * Page 42.........One.
                                                    * Page 49.........Unavoidable.
                                                    * Page 50.........Tipperary

13). ROYEAL JONES..........................*Page 51.........Shadow
    ALBUQUERQUE, NEW MEXICO

Well, I Have

Always Been

Told, I Have

To Say Something At

The End Of My Book.

So Ok, I Say

The End

Made in the USA
Middletown, DE
08 October 2023